# Inside the Mind of George Bernard Shaw

## DAVID GRAHAM

# DISCLAIMER

Although every effort has been taken to ensure all information in this book is accurate, human error is always a possibility and therefore the author apologises in the event of any inaccuracies.

# CONTENTS

# INTRODUCTION

Although known best for being one of the most prolific playwrights of the 19th and 20th centuries, George Bernard Shaw was notable for much more than this, and is without doubt one of the most interesting characters of his times.

Shaw began professional life as a critic of music and literature, before moving on to drama, ultimately writing more than sixty plays, as well as several novels and short stories. His works reflected his thoughts on many societal issues, including social inequality, religion, politics and marriage. The light touches of comedy that shone through his plays undoubtedly contributed towards their appeal to the masses.

Shaw was also passionate about politics; a staunch socialist, he devoted much of his life to the promotion of equal rights for all campaigned extensively against the exploitations of the lower classes of society. He was also a particularly humble individual; though he remains the only person to have won both the Nobel Prize for Literature and an Academy Award, he declined to accept all other awards, including the offer of a knighthood.

As one would expect from such a prolific writer (he is known to have written more than 250,000 letters during his lifetime), Shaw's has been quoted in abundance, both during his life and since his death in 1950.

This book brings together some of the most notable of his quotes on a variety of topics, providing a unique insight into the mind of this admirable character.

# ABOUT HIMSELF

"I never resist temptation, because I have found that things that are bad for me do not tempt me."

*

"I dislike feeling at home when I am abroad."

*

"I enjoy convalescence. It is the part that makes the illness worth while."

*

"Americans adore me and will go on adoring me until I say something nice about them."

\*

"I am a Christian. That obliges me to be a Communist."

\*

"When I was young, I observed that nine out of ten things I did were failures. So I did ten times more work."

\*

"I often quote myself. It adds spice to my conversation."

\*

"My reputation grows with every failure."

\*

"I want to be thoroughly used up when I die, for the harder I work the more I live. I rejoice in life for its own sake."

\*

"I learned long ago, never to wrestle with a pig. You get dirty, and besides, the pig likes it."

\*

"All my life affection has been showered upon me, and every forward step I have made has been taken in spite of it."

\*

"Animals are my friends... and I don't eat my friends."

\*

"You see things; and you say 'Why?' But I dream things that never were; and I say 'Why not?'"

*

"Few people think more than two or three times a year; I have made an international reputation for myself by thinking once or twice a week."

# ABOUT MANKIND

"The worst sin toward our fellow creatures is not to hate them, but to be indifferent to them: that's the essence of inhumanity."

\*

"The things most people want to know about are usually none of their business."

\*

"Beware of the man who does not return your blow: he neither forgives you nor allows you to forgive yourself."

\*

"Man can climb to the highest summits, but he cannot dwell there long."

\*

"When a stupid man is doing something he is ashamed of, he always declares that it is his duty."

\*

"A gentleman is one who puts more into the world than he takes out."

\*

"Few of us have vitality enough to make any of our instincts imperious."

\*

"The people who get on in this world are the people who get up and look for the circumstances they want and if they can't find them, make them."

*

"What a man believes may be ascertained, not from his creed, but from the assumptions on which he habitually acts."

*

"Men have to do some awfully mean things to keep up their respectability."

*

"A man of great common sense and good taste - meaning thereby a man without originality or moral courage."

*

"Except during the nine months before he draws his first breath, no man manages his affairs as well as a tree does."

*

"Liberty means responsibility. That is why most men dread it."

*

"A man never tells you anything until you contradict him."

*

"Men are wise in proportion, not to their experience, but to their capacity for experience."

*

"Human beings are the only animals of which I am thoroughly and cravenly afraid."

*

"Only on paper has humanity yet achieved glory, beauty, truth, knowledge, virtue, and abiding love."

\*

"Old men are dangerous: it doesn't matter to them what is going to happen to the world."

\*

"No man who is occupied in doing a very difficult thing, and doing it very well, ever loses his self-respect."

\*

"People become attached to their burdens sometimes more than the burdens are attached to them."

\*

"One man that has a mind and knows it can always beat ten men who haven't and don't."

\*

"Give a man health and a course to steer, and he'll

never stop to trouble about whether he's happy or not."

*

"If history repeats itself, and the unexpected always happens, how incapable must Man be of learning from experience."

*

"You'll never have a quiet world till you knock the patriotism out of the human race."

*

"Home life is no more natural to us than a cage is natural to a cockatoo."

*

"We are all dependent on one another, every soul of us on earth."

*

"Every man over forty is a scoundrel."

# FAMILY

"The natural term of the affection of the human animal for its offspring is six years."

*

"I am afraid we must make the world honest before we can honestly say to our children that honesty is the best policy."

*

"Perhaps the greatest social service that can be rendered by anybody to the country and to mankind is to bring up a family."

*

"Parentage is a very important profession, but no test of fitness for it is ever imposed in the interest of the children."

*

"If you must hold yourself up to your children as an object lesson, hold yourself up as a warning and not as an example."

*

"Never fret for an only son, the idea of failure will never occur to him."

# HUMOROUS

"It's easier to replace a dead man than a good
picture."

*

"England and America are two countries separated by
the same language."

*

"When a man says money can do anything, that
settles it: he hasn't got any."

*

"Life does not cease to be funny when people die any more than it ceases to be serious when people laugh."

*

"Better never than late."

*

"Hell is full of musical amateurs."

*

"He who can, does. He who cannot, teaches."

*

"If you can't get rid of the skeleton in your closet, you'd best teach it to dance."

*

"Which painting in the National Gallery would I save if there was a fire? The one nearest the door of course."

*

"I would like to take you seriously, but to do so would be an affront to your intelligence."

*

"Youth is a wonderful thing. What a crime to waste it on children."

*

"The secret to success is to offend the greatest number of people."

*

"The trouble with her is that she lacks the power of conversation but not the power of speech."

*

"An asylum for the sane would be empty in America."

*

"It is dangerous to be sincere unless you are also stupid."

# MARRIAGE & RELATIONSHIPS

"Marriage is popular because it combines the maximum of temptation with the maximum of opportunity."

*

"It is most unwise for people in love to marry."

*

"The test of a man or woman's breeding is how they behave in a quarrel."

*

"The perfect love affair is one which is conducted entirely by post."

*

"Marriage is an alliance entered into by a man who can't sleep with the window shut, and a woman who can't sleep with the window open."

*

"There is no subject on which more dangerous nonsense is talked and thought than marriage."

*

"Marriage is good enough for the lower classes: they have facilities for desertion that are denied to us."

*

"It is a curious sensation: the sort of pain that goes mercifully beyond our powers of feeling. When your heart is broken, your boats are burned: nothing matters any more. It is the end of happiness and the beginning of peace."

\*

"The fickleness of the women I love is only equalled by the infernal constancy of the women who love me."

\*

"A broken heart is a very pleasant complaint for a man in London if he has a comfortable income."

\*

"What is virtue but the Trade Unionism of the married?"

\*

"If women were particular about men's characters, they would never get married at all."

DAVID GRAHAM

# OPINIONS ON VARIOUS TOPICS

"Alcohol is the anesthesia by which we endure the operation of life."

*

"It is the mark of a truly intelligent person to be moved by statistics."

*

"Reading made Don Quixote a gentleman, but believing what he read made him mad."

*

"There is no sincerer love than the love of food."

\*

"Assassination is the extreme form of censorship."

\*

"A perpetual holiday is a good working definition of hell."

\*

"A man who has no office to go to, I don't care who he is, is a trial of which you can have no conception."

\*

"A veteran journalist has never had time to think twice before he writes."

\*

"Love is a gross exaggeration of the difference between one person and everybody else."

*

"Why, except as a means of livelihood, a man should desire to act on the stage when he has the whole world to act in, is not clear to me."

*

"We should all be obliged to appear before a board every five years and justify our existence... on pain of liquidation."

*

"An Englishman thinks he is moral when he is only uncomfortable."

*

"Censorship ends in logical completeness when nobody is allowed to read any books except the books that nobody reads."

*

"Science never solves a problem without creating ten more."

*

"The great advantage of a hotel is that it is a refuge from home life."

*

"Statistics show that of those who contract the habit of eating, very few survive."

*

"We are the only real aristocracy in the world: the aristocracy of money."

*

"The secret of being miserable is to have leisure to

bother about whether you are happy or not. The cure for it is occupation."

*

"Dancing is a perpendicular expression of a horizontal desire."

*

"There is no satisfaction in hanging a man who does not object to it."

*

"The British soldier can stand up to anything except the British War Office."

*

"Independence? That's middle class blasphemy. We are all dependent on one another, every soul of us on earth."

*

"What we want is to see the child in pursuit of knowledge, and not knowledge in pursuit of the child."

*

"There is nothing more dangerous than the conscience of a bigot."

*

"Property is organized robbery."

*

"Kings are not born: they are made by artificial hallucination."

*

"Patriotism is your conviction that this country is superior to all others because you were born in it."

*

"If all the economists were laid end to end, they'd
never reach a conclusion."

*

"Baseball has the great advantage over cricket of
being sooner ended."

*

"Without art, the crudeness of reality would make the
world unbearable."

*

"The moment we want to believe something, we
suddenly see all the arguments for it, and become
blind to the arguments against it."

*

"Cruelty would be delicious if one could only find
some sort of cruelty that didn't really hurt."

*

"You can always tell an old soldier by the inside of his holsters and cartridge boxes. The young ones carry pistols and cartridges; the old ones, grub."

# PHILOSOPHY

"You use a glass mirror to see your face; you use works of art to see your soul."

*

"Martyrdom: The only way a man can become famous without ability."

*

"There are no secrets better kept than the secrets everybody guesses."

*

"If there was nothing wrong in the world there wouldn't be anything for us to do."

*

"Very few people can afford to be poor."

*

"A life spent making mistakes is not only more honorable, but more useful than a life spent doing nothing."

*

"An index is a great leveller."

*

"A happy family is but an earlier heaven."

*

"Life contains but two tragedies. One is not to get your heart's desire; the other is to get it."

\*

"You cannot be a hero without being a coward."

\*

"I have to live for others and not for myself: that's middle-class morality."

\*

"The minority is sometimes right; the majority always wrong."

\*

"Those who do not know how to live must make a merit of dying."

\*

"Take care to get what you like or you will be forced
to like what you get."

*

"Self-sacrifice enables us to sacrifice other people
without blushing."

*

"Success does not consist in never making mistakes
but in never making the same one a second time."

*

"Lack of money is the root of all evil."

*

"The single biggest problem in communication is the
illusion that it has taken place."

*

"In heaven an angel is nobody in particular."

\*

"In this world there is always danger for those who
are afraid of it."

\*

"Life isn't about finding yourself. Life is about
creating yourself."

\*

"Just do what must be done. This may not be
happiness, but it is greatness."

\*

"Syllables govern the world."

\*

"Nothing is worth doing unless the consequences may be serious."

\*

"Oh, the tiger will love you. There is no sincerer love than the love of food."

\*

"Progress is impossible without change, and those who cannot change their minds cannot change anything."

\*

"All great truths begin as blasphemies."

\*

"Virtue consists, not in abstaining from vice, but in not desiring it."

\*

"We are made wise not by the recollection of our past, but by the responsibility for our future."

\*

"There are two tragedies in life. One is to lose your heart's desire. The other is to gain it."

\*

"The only secrets are the secrets that keep themselves."

\*

"The golden rule is that there are no golden rules."

\*

"Miracles, in the sense of phenomena we cannot explain, surround us on every hand: life itself is the miracle of miracles."

\*

"You have learnt something. That always feels at first as if you had lost something."

\*

"The liar's punishment is not in the least that he is not believed, but that he cannot believe anyone else."

\*

"Silence is the most perfect expression of scorn."

\*

"The possibilities are numerous once we decide to act and not react."

\*

"A little learning is a dangerous thing, but we must take that risk because a little is as much as our biggest heads can hold."

*

"Everything happens to everybody sooner or later if there is time enough."

*

"Virtue is insufficient temptation."

*

"Beauty is a short-lived tyranny."

*

"People who say it cannot be done should not interrupt those who are doing it."

*

"The only way to avoid being miserable is not to have enough leisure to wonder whether you are happy or not."

\*

"The faults of the burglar are the qualities of the financier."

\*

"A fool's brain digests philosophy into folly, science into superstition, and art into pedantry. Hence University education."

\*

"Better keep yourself clean and bright; you are the window through which you must see the world."

\*

"Beware of false knowledge; it is more dangerous than ignorance."

\*

"Life would be tolerable but for its amusements."

\*

"We don't stop playing because we grow old; we grow old because we stop playing."

\*

"We learn from experience that men never learn anything from experience."

\*

"First love is only a little foolishness and a lot of curiosity."

\*

"The power of accurate observation is commonly called cynicism by those who have not got it."

\*

"We must always think about things, and we must think about things as they are, not as they are said to be."

\*

"Every person who has mastered a profession is a skeptic concerning it."

\*

"Life levels all men. Death reveals the eminent."

\*

"The man with a toothache thinks everyone happy whose teeth are sound. The poverty-stricken man makes the same mistake about the rich man."

\*

"Hegel was right when he said that we learn from history that man can never learn anything from history."

\*

"You are going to let the fear of poverty govern you life and your reward will be that you will eat, but you will not live."

*

"The man who writes about himself and his own time is the only man who writes about all people and about all time."

*

"Peace is not only better than war, but infinitely more arduous."

*

"The only service a friend can really render is to keep up your courage by holding up to you a mirror in which you can see a noble image of yourself."

*

"Choose silence of all virtues, for by it you hear other men's imperfections, and conceal your own."

*

"We have no more right to consume happiness without producing it than to consume wealth without producing it."

*

"In a battle all you need to make you fight is a little hot blood and the knowledge that it's more dangerous to lose than to win."

*

"If you injure your neighbour, better not do it by halves."

*

"Fashions, after all, are only induced epidemics."

*

"It's so hard to know what to do when one wishes
earnestly to do right."

\*

"When a man wants to murder a tiger he calls it sport;
when a tiger wants to murder him he calls it ferocity."

\*

"The truth is, hardly any of us have ethical energy
enough for more than one really inflexible point of
honor."

\*

"Nothing is ever done in this world until men are
prepared to kill one another if it is not done."

\*

"Do not try to live forever. You will not succeed."

\*

"If you leave the smallest corner of your head vacant
for a moment, other people's opinions will rush in
from all quarters."

*

"While we ourselves are the living graves of murdered
animals, how can we expect any ideal living
conditions on this earth?"

*

"Imagination is the beginning of creation. You
imagine what you desire, you will what you imagine
and at last you create what you will."

*

"No question is so difficult to answer as that to which
the answer is obvious."

*

"Youth is wasted on the young."

*

"Use your health, even to the point of wearing it out. That is what it is for. Spend all you have before you die; do not outlive yourself."

*

"Do not do unto others as you expect they should do unto you. Their tastes may not be the same."

*

"Beauty is all very well at first sight; but who ever looks at it when it has been in the house three days?"

*

"I never thought much of the courage of a lion tamer. Inside the cage he is at least safe from people."

# POLITICS

"Capitalism has destroyed our belief in any effective power but that of self interest backed by force."

*

"Democracy is a form of government that substitutes election by the incompetent many for appointment by the corrupt few."

*

"The love of economy is the root of all virtue."

*

"A government that robs Peter to pay Paul can always depend on the support of Paul."

\*

"Do not waste your time on Social Questions. What is the matter with the poor is Poverty; what is the matter with the rich is Uselessness."

\*

"Power does not corrupt men; fools, however, if they get into a position of power, corrupt power."

\*

"Clever and attractive women do not want to vote; they are willing to let men govern as long as they govern men."

\*

"What Englishman will give his mind to politics as long as he can afford to keep a motor car?"

\*

"Political necessities sometime turn out to be political mistakes."

\*

"Democracy is a device that insures we shall be governed no better than we deserve."

\*

"Until the men of action clear out the talkers we who have social consciences are at the mercy of those who have none."

\*

"The art of government is the organisation of idolatry."

\*

"He knows nothing and thinks he knows everything. That points clearly to a political career."

*

"Democracy substitutes election by the incompetent many for appointment by the corrupt few."

*

"Find enough clever things to say, and you're a Prime Minister; write them down and you're a Shakespeare."

*

"The first condition of progress is the removal of censorship."

*

"An election is a moral horror, as bad as a battle except for the blood; a mud bath for every soul concerned in it."

*

"Socialism is the same as Communism, only better English."

DAVID GRAHAM

# RELIGION

"The heretic is always better dead. And mortal eyes cannot distinguish the saint from the heretic."

\*

"The frontier between hell and heaven is only the difference between two ways of looking at things."

\*

"The best place to find God is in a garden. You can dig for him there."

\*

"No man ever believes that the Bible means what it says: He is always convinced that it says what he means."

\*

"Why should we take advice on sex from the pope? If he knows anything about it, he shouldn't!"

\*

"I'm an atheist and I thank God for it."

\*

"There is only one religion, though there are a hundred versions of it."

\*

"Most people do not pray; they only beg."

\*

"The fact that a believer is happier than a skeptic is no more to the point than the fact that a drunken man is happier than a sober one."

DAVID GRAHAM

# ALSO BY DAVID GRAHAM

The Very Best of Ralph Waldo Emerson

The Very Best of Clint Eastwood

The Very Best of Roger Moore

The Very Best of Kirk Douglas